The Fight For Joy

Written and published by
Josh Bruckerhoff

Contents

The Fight for Joy

Sing, my child, sing

I remember it like it was yesterday. A special moment was shared between my oldest daughter and me. She absolutely loves listening to *"Princess Music"* (which is really a station on one of the apps on my phone), while riding in the car. A song came on from one of her favorite movies, and she wailed it out. She was singing as loud as she could. She didn't know all of the words; she didn't care. She sang as loud as she could, and as she did this... a few things I noticed:

She didn't care that she wasn't on key.

She didn't care that she didn't know all of the words.

She sang for the song.

It was music to my ears, *"Sing, Brinkley, Sing..."* I said over and over. *"Sing, Brinkley, Sing..."*

Then I realized...

I'd lost the song.

I'd lost the celebration.

I'd lost the joy.

I'd been so wrapped up in the work of sobriety and recovery that I hadn't given myself the time to celebrate it. I'd traded the chains of alcoholism and drug addiction for chains of slave labor. I remember saying to myself, *"It feels like I'm always rushing from one place to another. I can't seem to stop... and I'm so tired."*

Maybe it had to do with my mind. Before sobriety, many of my celebratory occasions would include my consumption of a lot of alcohol. Perhaps in my brain, there was a connection between the two.

Before sobriety, when I needed to relax, I would take a pain or sleeping pill, or drink alcohol. Perhaps in my brain, there is some sort of connection.

Could it be that my brain was saying, that since

alcohol and drugs were a big part of my celebratory and relaxing experiences and they no longer were, that now I was unable to relax or celebrate? Because I'd done neither in quite some time.

How did I celebrate and relax before the alcohol and drugs?

And don't get me wrong... I did have much to celebrate, and God had taken care of me enough that I should celebrate His victories and be content in His provision. But knowing and having are very different.

I'm going to dig a bit deeper on this in the next few chapters.

A good friend of mine once said, *"In our society, it's easy to be cynical. It's joy that we have to fight for."*

And as I write this, I remember hearing a heartbroken God say, *"Sing, my child, sing."*

> *"Daddy, I want to, but I don't know the words. I need to, but I can't find the note. Daddy, that*

other guy sings much better than I do, I'm sure you'd be better pleased with his song.

Daddy, I can't sing right now, I really want to, really I do, You know I do. Daddy, please help me to find...

not the words...

not the notes...

but the song."

And I can still hear God today saying, "*Sing, my child, sing.*"

Sing, my child, sing

Application: What is God saying to me?

The Fight for Joy

<u>Party or die</u>

> *"I like to picture Jesus in a tuxedo T-Shirt because it says I want to be formal, but I'm here to party too.*
>
> *Because I like to party, and I like my Jesus to party."*
>
> - Cal Naughton Jr, Talladega Nights

Last chapter, I wrote about a dilemma that I remember facing.

It seemed that I'd lost my ability to celebrate life. I'd worked extremely hard in my recovery, but in my working, I'd failed to celebrate what God had done for me. Because there is always more work to be done, isn't there?

One of the main metaphors that God uses in describing His kingdom, His people and His purpose in the world is a party. But all too often, many of us have church experiences more similar to a funeral.

This was never God's intention.

Actually in Leviticus 23, God says that a person's failure to join in the Passover celebration was punishable by death. And Passover wasn't some boring tea party. *(No offense to those who like tea)*

At Passover, the Jewish people were commanded to bring 10% of everything they had made that year and pretty much blow it all on this gigantic celebration of what God had done for them.

The theme of celebration is all throughout Scripture and all throughout Jesus's life in the Gospels. Jesus was even called a glutton and a drunkard, not because He was, but because He celebrated life in a way that made other people notice.

I'd like to end this chapter with a question.

What is the application for Jesus turning the water into wine? I get all of His other miracles, but this one is challenging. John writes at the end of his Gospel, that there were so many things that Jesus said and did that John had to pick and choose what he wrote. So why did he write about Jesus turning the water into wine? And furthermore, why did he skip over Christ's birth, baptism and temptation to include it at the very beginning of his Gospel?

John is the only Gospel writer to include this miracle and there is a reason, and I'll go into that in the next chapter.

I can't wait to unpack this, but for now I must stop here.

Party or die

Application: What is God saying to me?

The Fight for Joy

Alcohol or not, it's still a party

All throughout the Bible, wine is synonymous with celebration. Wine symbolizes God's abundance, joy, shalom, peace, and the Day that He returns and makes everything right. In fact it was believed that when the Messiah came, there would be a wedding, and He would bring with Him a lot of wine.

> *"On this mountain the Lord Almighty will prepare a feast of rich food for all peoples, a banquet of aged wine - the best of meats and the finest of wines."* - Isaiah 25

> *"They will come and shout for joy on the heights of Zion; they will rejoice in the bounty of the Lord-the grain, the new wine and the oil, the young of the flock and herds. They will be like a well-watered garden, and they will sorrow no more."* - Jeremiah 31

This concept is hard for many of us to grasp, because our culture takes advantage of alcohol. Many of us have experienced...

Abuse from an alcoholic family member...

An accident caused by intoxication...

Death...

Pain...

Wounds...

All due to the abuse of alcohol.

This has been my experience. A disconnect from reality, a way to numb (not heal) my pain. To be the Superman I wanted to be. Putting family on an altar built to the god of intoxication.

But drunkenness wasn't the case in Jesus's culture. In the days when this miracle took place, getting drunk on wine was extremely rare and looked down upon. It was seen as taking advantage of God's good gift, His shalom or blessing, and could shame the individual for a lifetime. Another reason is that Israel was a dry country *(Not to be confused with a dry county).* Water was rationed, and wine was scarce, only reserved for the wealthiest of their culture... except at weddings.

Which brings us to the Gospel of John, where Jesus is at a wedding that runs out of wine.

> *On the third day a wedding took place at Cana in Galilee. Jesus' mother was there,and Jesus and his disciples had also been invited to the wedding. When the wine was gone, Jesus' mother said to him, "They have no more wine."*
>
> *"Dear woman, why do you involve me?" Jesus replied, "My time has not yet come."His mother said to the servants, "Do whatever he tells you."*
>
> *Nearby stood six stone water jars, the kind used by the Jews for ceremonial washing, each holding from twenty to thirty gallons.*
>
> *Jesus said to the servants, "Fill the jars with water"; so they filled them to the brim.*

Then he told them, "Now draw some out and take it to the master of the banquet."

They did so, and the master of the banquet tasted the water that had been turned into wine. He did not realize where it had come from, though the servants who had drawn the water knew. Then he called the bridegroom aside and said, "Everyone brings out the choice wine first and then the cheaper wine after the guests have had too much to drink; but you have saved the best till now."

This, the first of his miraculous signs, Jesus performed in Cana of Galilee. He thus revealed his glory, and his disciples put their faith in him. - John 2

"When the wine was gone..." We have no idea what these words meant. This was an honor shame society, which meant that the best thing that could happen was for someone to be honored publicly or to have saved face. But the worst thing that could happen would be public shame.

Running out of wine would've been a huge public shame.

Remember, a Jewish wedding represented God's deliverance from Egypt and the Messiah's return to set the world right. It lasted 7 days and was an event that people would travel long distances to attend. Wine was scarce and expensive, which meant that parents saved for years in order to supply their guests with wine for the day their children would wed. Because they wanted to make sure in the celebration that everyone had wine, or the blessing of God.

This would've been a social catastrophe that brought shame on the parents for a lifetime; and could even be seen as putting a curse on the marriage.

So Mary goes to Jesus and tells Him about the situation. And the servants fill 6 ceremonial cleansing jars with water. And the master confronts the bride and groom and praises them for the quality of the wine that they have saved. This was about 150 gallons of wine!

Shame to honor. All because of Jesus.

But John ends this story by calling the miracle a

sign. Signs in the Bible were always something that pointed to something else.

In the next chapter I'll talk about another party that John directly contrasts to this one.

Alcohol or not, it's still a party

Application: What is God saying to me?

The Fight for Joy

Crashing the party

Every Gospel has the story of Jesus turning over the tables in the temple, and every Gospel writer includes this story at the end of their book. In fact, it is a big motivation for the religious rulers wanting to crucify Jesus.

But John doesn't write this story at the end of his Gospel. He puts it right after Jesus's turning the water into wine, at the beginning of Jesus's ministry.

> *After this he went down to Capernaum with his mother and brothers and his disciples. There they stayed for a few days.*
>
> *When it was almost time for the Jewish Passover, Jesus went up to Jerusalem. In the temple courts he found men selling cattle, sheep and doves, and others sitting at tables exchanging money. So he made a whip out of cords, and drove all from the temple area, both sheep and cattle; he scattered the coins of the money changers and overturned their*

tables. To those who sold doves he said, "Get these out of here! How dare you turn my Father's house into a market!"

His disciples remembered that it is written: "Zeal for your house will consume me."

Then the Jews demanded of him, "What miraculous sign can you show us to prove your authority to do all this?"

Jesus answered them, "Destroy this temple, and I will raise it again in three days."

The Jews replied, "It has taken forty-six years to build this temple, and you are going to raise it in three days?" But the temple he had spoken of was his body. After he was raised from the dead, his disciples recalled what he had said. Then they believed the Scripture and the words that Jesus had spoken.

Now while he was in Jerusalem at the Passover Feast, many people saw the miraculous signs he was doing and believed in his name. But Jesus would not entrust himself to them, for he knew all

> *men. He did not need man's testimony about man, for he knew what was in a man.* – John 2

It's not an accident that John puts both of these stories together. I think John is trying to tell us what Jesus's kingdom looks like, and what it doesn't.

A bit about the temple sacrifices of that day...

The Sadducees weren't supposed to manage the temple, the Levites were. But when Caesar came into power, he held an auction selling the role of managing the temple to the highest bidder. The Sadducees in their wealth, bought the right. And they came up with a fantastic idea... to take advantage of worship.

Coins of that day had the face of Caesar on it. Caesar considered himself a god. The Sadducees said that they wouldn't allow any image of false gods in the temple. So they would exchange "Caesar money" in for "temple money". This happened in the temple courts. Anyone who needed to purchase an animal for sacrifice had to make the purchase at an exorbitant exchange rate. Some scholars say the exchange was 10 to 1.

The rich were taking advantage of the poor, the powerful taking advantage of the powerless. They were taking advantage of peoples' guilt, shame and requirement for sacrifice and turning a big profit. And business was good. They were holding people to rules that had to be followed in order to obtain forgiveness.

Rules...

Rules...

Rules...

And Jesus shows up and wrecks shop. Not because He is against rules, but because He wants to be served out of love and not requirement. And the most interesting thing about this story...

John says that it occurred at Passover, the biggest party on the Jewish calendar.

John starts Jesus' ministry by comparing parties.

It's as if John is saying that the Kingdom is not about being bound, tied down and taken advantage of by our own guilt and shame. The kingdom is about turning our shame and guilt into joy, celebration and honor.

And He does all of this at a party.

Shame to honor, all because of Jesus.

Sounds good, but this all happened two thousand years ago. What does this have to do with us?

I'll talk about that next.

Crashing the party

Application: What is God saying to me?

The Fight for Joy

<u>Getting our party on</u>

In this post I will try to make application for the passage of Jesus's party experience.

There are 5 things that are very interesting in the story about the water being turned into wine.

<u>The Wedding</u>:
Weddings represent God's relationship with His people. In the Old Testament God is constantly referred to as the groom, and His people the Bride. Even today, Jewish wedding language is the same Old Testament love language between God the Israelites. The wedding also represented the Kingdom of God.

Interesting that all this is happening at a wedding.

<u>The First Four Words</u>:
"On the third day..." What else happened on a third day? The resurrection.

When the readers of John saw this, their ears

perked up. They knew where John was going with this. He included this purposefully. Directly tied in to an elaborate wedding party where shame was turned into honor, John is pointing to the resurrection.

It is as if John is saying that the resurrection is changing the entire mind set of what the Kingdom looks like, that it is more like a party than a religious ceremony.

<u>The Jars</u>:

One thing we must know about the jars. The Bible says they were used for ceremonial cleansing. This was the same water that the guests had washed their hands in, water that was filthy in jars that represented cleanliness. And Jesus uses this water, nasty water comparable to toilet water, and turns it into wine.

John isn't saying that cleansing isn't important. Jesus is all about cleaning the hearts of His people, but what Jesus uses in this story isn't clean water.

Jesus uses the dirt, the filth, the grime of our lives,

and He uses it to introduce the world to the greatest party of all. He uses it to turn a situation of public shame into a situation of honor. And many churches are failing in this cause.

It is so easy to hide our shame, our sin, our filthiness, isn't it? And religious self-righteousness only promotes this guilt. But no one can relate to pure righteousness, can they? Because none of us are. Only by embracing our weaknesses, wounds and struggles, are we able to share in God's story for our lives and the lives of others.

Revealing His Glory:
At the end of John's story of Jesus turning water into wine, John mentions Jesus revealing God's glory. This is a loaded statement to the Jewish people. Because the glory of God was reserved for the temple. God came down and filled the temple, but not in this instance.

John is saying that the story of God is a lot less than a religion and a lot more like a party.

When we realize just how the kingdom of God is, the only appropriate response is to celebrate.

The Servants:

The passage never says, *"And then Jesus turned the water into wine..."* He did, but I don't think that is the emphasis here. The servants simply obeyed, and the party was saved.

The Screwtape Letters is one of my favorite books written by CS Lewis. The book is written as a series of letters from a devil named Screwtape to his nephew, Wormwood, about how to woo a Christian away from God (Make sure to keep that in mind as you are reading the quotes, especially if you're wondering why God is referred to as "The Enemy.")

> *"Never forget that when we are dealing with any pleasure in its healthy and normal and satisfying form, we are, in a sense, on the Enemy's ground. I know we have won many a soul through pleasure. All the same, it is His invention, not ours. He made all the pleasures: all our research so far has not enabled us to produce one. All we can do is to encourage the humans to take pleasures which our Enemy has produced, at times, or in ways, or in degrees, which He has forbidden. Hence we always try to work away*

from the natural condition of any pleasure to that in which it is least natural, least redolent of its Maker, and least pleasurable." -- P.41-42

This is the problem with church and our culture.

We have let the world define so narrowly what a party should be.

Think about it. Most anytime we hear about a Christian at a party, it's a negative thing, right? But Jesus was commonly referred to as a drunkard and a glutton by the religious leaders of His day, not because He was, but because they had forgotten who they were called to be. So why to the world does Christianity seem more like a funeral than a party?

Christianity has become so anti-party, hasn't it?

Young people, if they're honest, will tell you that their reason for not accepting Christ is that they want to have fun. But Christians, if they look like Jesus, should have the market cornered on fun. No Super Bowl party, Emmy or Grammy party should hold a candle to the Church's celebrations.

It's about time the church got its party on. Think of it this way. We eat cake to celebrate a day when there will be no hungry. We laugh and shout to celebrate a day when there will be no more crying. We dance to celebrate a day when wheelchairs will no longer be needed. We embrace life to celebrate a day when there will be no more funerals.

Now…I'm off to a party!

Getting our party on

Application: What is God saying to me?

The Author

Josh Bruckerhoff is a Christian, husband, father, son, brother and friend. He resides in Dallas, Texas. Josh holds a degree in Church Ministries and has served as both Worship and Youth Minister, in addition to teaching ministry classes and leading small groups. Josh has a unique style of delivering the message of Christ in a way that is relevant and applicable to everyone who hears it. He believes that being a Christian is not a destination, but a journey; and he respects the fact that all believers aren't at the same place in that journey. His message is one that is tailored to people where they are in life.

Josh has a passion for seeing others live up to their full potential in Christ. He desires that people realize the gifts that God has put inside of them so that they can share them to enrich the lives of others. Understanding that God doesn't live in our world, but that we live in His, Josh encourages others to share Christ, not only in words, but in relationships.

Josh enjoys sharing his thoughts and experiences on his website: www.thekidtheking.com.

For more information, he can be contacted at Josh@thekidtheking.com

www.ingramcontent.com/pod-product-compliance
Ingram Content Group UK Ltd.
Pitfield, Milton Keynes, MK11 3LW, UK
UKHW020215250726
13967UKWH00001B/11

9 781300 921981